50 THINGS YOU DIDN'T KNOW ABOUT

FRANCE

Written and Illustrated
by Sean O'Neill

RED CHAIR PRESS

Egremont, Massachusetts

50 Things You Didn't Know About is produced and published by Red Chair Press:
www.redchairpress.com

FREE lesson guide at www.redchairpress.com/free-activities

Publisher's Cataloging-In-Publication Data

(Provided by Cassidy Cataloging Services, Inc)

Names: O'Neill, Sean, 1968- author, illustrator. | O'Neill, Sean, 1968 50 things you didn't know about (Series)

Title: 50 things you didn't know about France / written and illustrated by Sean O'Neill.

Other Titles: France

Description: Egremont, Massachusetts : Red Chair Press, [2024] | Interest age level: 006-009. | Includes bibliographical references and index. | Summary: With 50 Things You Didn't Know About France, young readers will discover the highlights of France's history and royal rulers, modern traditions as well as strange and unusual laws, and discover unique aspects of food and daily life in France.-- Publisher.

Identifiers: ISBN: 978-1-64371-336-6 (library hardcover) | 978-1-64371-337-3 (softcover) | 978-1-64371-338-0 (ebook) | LCCN: 2023936980

Subjects: LCSH: France--History--Juvenile literature. | France--Description and travel--Juvenile literature. | France--Social life and customs--Juvenile literature. | CYAC: France--History. | France--Description and travel. | France--Social life and customs. | BISAC: JUVENILE NONFICTION / Travel. | JUVENILE NONFICTION / People & Places / Europe.

Classification: LCC: DC17 .O54 2024 | DDC: 944--dc23

Printed in the United States of America

0524 1P F24CG

TABLE of CONTENTS

Chapter 1:
HISTORY 4

Chapter 2:
REVOLUTION AND EMPIRE 10

Chapter 3:
LEGENDS AND TRADITIONS 14

Chapter 4:
DAILY LIFE 22

Chapter 5:
CULTURE AND CUISINE 26

Glossary 30

Explore More 31

Index/About the Author 32

CHAPTER 1

HISTORY

Located smack dab in the middle of the continent, France is Europe's largest country* and, for centuries, has been at the crossroads of history. Surrounded by seas on 3 sides and protected by mountains, France's rich farmland, mild climate, and natural borders has made it a natural home for great civilizations throughout its history. From its prehistoric beginnings, through monarchy, revolution, empire, and democracy, the history of France is a sweeping saga, and sometimes a bumpy ride.

*Members of the European Union.

1 The earliest known inhabitants of what we now call France were a tribe of early humans called Celts (or Les Gaulois in French). They called their land *Gaul*, which is derived from a Celtic word for "hero."

2 The Celts also named the French capital, Paris. The city was built around a small island in the Seine river, and the earliest inhabitants were boaters and fishermen. The Celtic word for boat is *par*, so the people were called the *parisii*– boat people.

3 Around 100 B.C.E., the land of Gaul was conquered by the Romans. This invasion and occupation was a major victory for an up-and-coming Roman general who was headed for bigger things–Julius Caesar.

4 The name Gaul didn't really stick, but, after the Romans left, a new tribe of Germanic people arrived from the east. That tribe's name–the Franks–turned out to be a little more permanent. The Kingdom of the Franks eventually became known as *France.*

5 Before the Romans arrived, the Greeks settled and built a city in southern France called Massilia. It's now known as Marseilles, France's second largest city and one of its oldest.

6 The first Frankish King, Clovis, was crowned around 400 and is remembered as the first king of France. A more modern French translation of his name, *Louis*, became the name for 19 more French kings.

7 A few hundred years later, in about 800, another famous French king named Charlemagne would get his revenge on Julius Caesar. Under Charlemagne, the new Frankish empire conquered Rome and all of Italy. Take that Caesar!

8 In this period there were several French Kings with unusual titles, including Pepin the Short, Charles the Bald, Charles the Fat, and Charles the Simple.

9 In 1066, William the Conqueror from Normandy, in northern France, invaded England and became king. For the next 400 years northern France (including Paris) was officially part of England.

10 The Bayeaux Tapestry, a 230-foot-long medieval artwork, tells the story of the Norman invasion of England with over 70 scenes of battle sewn into linen. It's one of the greatest pieces of **medieval** art and is nearly 1,000 years old.

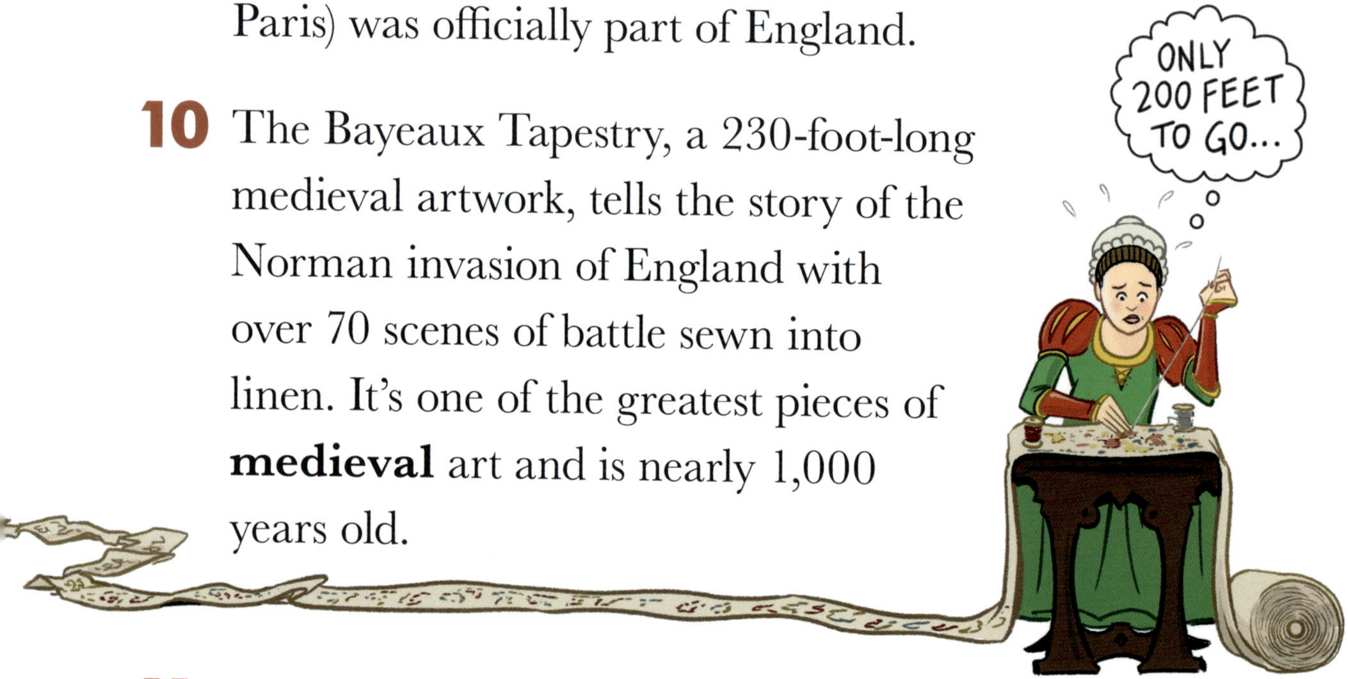

11 In 1429 a seventeen-year-old girl named Joan of Arc convinced the French King Charles VII, to let her lead an army against the English. She commanded a force of 4,000 men to defeat the English at the city of Orléans.

12 Joan of Arc's victory was so inspiring to the French that the English feared her symbolic power and captured her and burnt her at the stake.

13 Joan of Arc is remembered as a great hero in France. Her victories and inspiration led to the final defeat of the English in 1453. This event is remembered by historians as the birth of the modern nation of France.

CHAPTER 2

REVOLUTION AND EMPIRE

The glory of the French monarchy reached its peak in the 17th century with the reign of King Louis XIV. Known as the "Sun King," Louis built grand tributes to his wealth and power, including the huge palace of Versailles. But widespread poverty and anger toward the King soon boiled over, and in 1789, the French Revolution began, changing the history of France–and the world–forever.

14 The French Revolution marked the end of the monarchy in France–at least for a while. King Louis XVI (ruled 1754–1793) was forced from power and eventually beheaded in 1793, but his younger brother, Louis XVIII, returned to the throne 22 years later.

15 French queen, wife of Louis XVI, Marie Antoinette famously remarked, "let them eat cake," when asked about the starving peasants of France. But she didn't mean birthday cake–she was referring to the crumbs left behind in a bread pan after the wealthy had eaten all they wanted.

16 Louis was a very popular name for French kings. There were 19 of them, although King Louis XIX, one of the last French monarchs, stepped down after only 20 minutes on the throne, making him the shortest-reigning monarch in history.

17 One of the most important holidays in France is Bastille Day, July 14th. It marks the beginning of the French Revolution, when angry Parisians stormed the Bastille, a large prison for criminals and political enemies of the King.

18 The Revolution changed everything in France—including the calendar! The French Republican Calendar was adopted in 1793 and included a 10-day week called a *décadé* and all new months with names like *Nivôse* (snowy), *Pluviôse* (rainy) and *Floréal* (flowery). Napoleon changed the calendar back on January 1, 1806 to the pre-Revolutionary calendar we know today.

19 The Revolution began with the idea of liberty, equality, and **brotherhood**, but soon became a bloody Reign of Terror. During this period 250,000 French people were arrested and 30,000 beheaded by the dreaded *guillotine*.

20 Things got so bad that the leader of the Reign of Terror, Maximilien de Robespierre, was also beheaded in 1794.

21 After the Revolution and Reign of Terror, a popular general named Napoleon Bonaparte came to power to rule France. Napoleon's nickname was "the little colonel," even though he was actually a general.

22 Napoleon built an empire that spread throughout Europe and even into parts of Africa. In Egypt, soldiers from Napoleon's army discovered an ancient artifact called the Rosetta Stone, which allowed scholars to read Egyptian hieroglyphics for the first time.

23 Napoleon fell from power and was banished to an island called Elba. But he was able to escape and make one more attempt to rule France. His empire came to an end for good at the Battle of Waterloo in 1815.

CHAPTER 3

LEGENDS AND TRADITIONS

The nation of France and its people have a character all their own. The French are fiercely proud of their language, culture and traditions, even if some of them seem a little surprising to outsiders. But, as the French say, "*Vive la différence!*"

24 French people have given their country an unusual nickname: *l'Hexagone*. If you look at a map, you'll see that the country looks a bit like a five-sided hexagon.

25 Even though it only has five sides, France shares borders with eight different countries: Belgium, Germany, Italy, Luxembourg, Monaco, Spain, Switzerland, and Andorra.

26 In the middle of Paris is a small island in the Seine river called *Ile St. Louis.* Until 1614 nobody lived on the island, and it was mostly used for drying laundry and the occasional duel.

27 The hot-air balloon, one of the earliest methods of flight, was invented in France by the brothers Joseph and Jacques Montgolfier. Montgolfière is now the French name for a hot-air balloon.

28 Another French invention which stayed around a lot longer is the motion picture. The first movie was shown in 1895 in Paris. Made by the Lumiere brothers, the film showed a group of workers leaving a factory and was only five seconds long, but the moving images captured the imagination of Parisians.

29 The French have many unusual expressions involving animals. In France you may "cry like a cow," or be as scared as a "wet chicken." And if something is crazy, you can say *Oh! La vache* meaning *A cow!* or *OMG!*

30 Several familiar terms in English come from the French language. *Bon appétit, C'est la vie, déjà vu* and *tour de force* are all expressions that come from France.

31 Something else most people use every day–the camera phone–was invented in France. The first mobile phone picture was taken in Paris in 1997.

32 In France it's considered bad luck to turn a *baguette* (a loaf of French bread) upside-down. In medieval times it was said that a loaf of bread that was turned over was set aside for an executioner, and it's been bad luck ever since.

33 On April 1st the French have an April Fool's tradition of sticking a paper fish on your back and calling you an "April Fish."

34 There are some other unusual French laws on the books. Until 2013, it was officially illegal for women to wear pants in public.

35 If you're riding the train in France, don't try to kiss anyone goodbye–it's illegal! In 1910 a law was passed banning any kissing on train platforms. Apparently, the kiss goodbye was making the trains late.

36 The French flag is referred to as *le tricolore* or the three colors. The blue, white and red stripes represent the ideals of the French Revolution: liberté (liberty), égalité (equality), and fraternité (brotherhood).

CHAPTER 4

DAILY LIFE

The modern nation of France is home to over 60 million people. Centuries-old traditions of fishing and agriculture coexist with the bustling **cosmopolitan** flair of one of the world's most glamorous cities–Paris. Daily life in France can be sweet, surprising, and never dull.

37 France is the most visited country in the world, with almost 90 million tourists arriving each year.

38 France and England are separated by the English Channel, a body of water that is only 34 km (about 20 miles) at its shortest distance. Since 1994, travelers can ride a train across, or, actually, *under* the channel in the "chunnel," an underwater tunnel linking the two countries.

39 The image of a Frenchman wearing a beret may have come from French onion farmers in the 19th century who traveled across the English Channel to sell onions to the British. They wore rugged felt hats called *berets*, which made a big impression on their English customers.

40 One symbol of France is Paris's famous Eiffel Tower. When it was built in 1889 it was the world's tallest structure. It weighs more than 10,000 tons and has 1,665 steps.

41 If you make it to the top, you may find a secret room! The creator of the tower, Gustave Eiffel, created a secret apartment at the top of the Eiffel Tower which he used to entertain special guests.

42 Beneath the city of Paris is a system of caverns and catacombs (open tombs) that has existed for almost 2,000 years. Many of them contain mass graves of dead bodies from the Middle Ages.

43 Another landmark in Paris is the *Pont Neuf,* which means New Bridge. Kind of a funny name, considering the bridge is 400 years old.

44 The most popular sporting event in France, by far, is the Tour de France bicycle race, which covers 2,300 miles over three weeks. And it's not just popular in France. The Tour de France is the most watched sporting event in the world, with about 3.5 billion viewers tuning in.

CHAPTER

5

CULTURE AND CUISINE

If there's anything that the French value more than their delicious food traditions, it's their commitment to the arts and culture. On any given day, the cafés of Paris are filled with delicious pastries and discussions of politics, philosophy, and art. An appreciation of "the finer things" is part of the French character and identity, as these surprising facts demonstrate.

45 Have you ever eaten a snail? The French call them *escargot* and they eat a LOT of them–about 25,000 tons a year. That comes out to about 500 per person. Yum!

46 If you want to take any of those snails on a train, you'd better buy them a ticket. According to French law, domesticated animals–including snails–can't ride without paying a fare.

47 The French are known for their food, but two of the most famous French treats–the *baguette* and the *croissant*–originally came from Austria. Many French buy a fresh baguette every day.

48 The earliest known art created by humans are cave paintings made by prehistoric humans over 15,000 years ago, discovered in a cave in Lascaux, France.

49 The famous Louvre museum in Paris is the world's largest museum. It's estimated that if you looked at every piece of art in their collection for 30 seconds, it would take over six months to see everything.

50 The crow of a rooster and the ringing of a church bell at dawn. The rumble of a tractor and the smell of manure from stables. The buzzing of cicadas or the croaking of frogs. Quacking ducks, bleating sheep and braying donkeys. These are all now protected by law to preserve the rural heritage of France.

Glossary

brotherhood: when people work together for the same purpose, usually caring for each other (in French: fraternité)

cosmopolitan: having people from different countries and cultures mixed together in a place.

medieval: of the Middle Ages from the Fall of Rome to the Renaissance; from the 5th to the 15th Centuries

Explore More

Books

Deary, Terry. *Horrible Histories: France.* Scholastic, 2013.

Grack, Rachel. *France (Exploring Countries).* Bellwether Media, 2019.

Haley, Charly. *Your Passport to France.* Capstone Press, 2021.

Nnachi, Ngeri. *Spotlight on France.* Lerner Publications, 2024.

Van, R.L. *France.* Abdo Big Buddy Books, 2023.

Index

Bastille Day 12
Bayeaux Tapestry. 8
Charlemagne 7
Charles, King. 8
Clovis, King 6
Eiffel Tower 24
French Revolution 11–13
Gaul 5
Joan of Arc 8-9
Julius Caesar 5, 7
Lascaux 28
Louix XIV, King 10
Louvre 29
Marie Antoinette 11
Marseilles 6
Montgolfier, Jacques. 18
Napoleon Bonaparte 14–15
Paris 5, 17, 22, 25
Tour de France. 25
William the Conqueror 8

About the Author/Illustrator

Sean O'Neill is an illustrator and writer living in Chicago. He is the creator of the *Rocket Robinson* series of graphic novels. Sean loves traveling, history, trivia, and drawing cartoons, so this project is pretty much a dream assignment. And it comes with snails on the rails!